Real Estate Success Planner

Event Sign In Sheet

NAME: _____

EMAIL: _____

PHONE: _____

ARE YOU PRE-QUALIFIED?
☐ YES   ☐ NO
ARE YOU WORKING WITH AN AGENT?
☐ YES   ☐ NO

NAME: _____

EMAIL: _____

PHONE: _____

ARE YOU PRE-QUALIFIED?
☐ YES   ☐ NO
ARE YOU WORKING WITH AN AGENT?
☐ YES   ☐ NO

NAME: _____

EMAIL: _____

PHONE: _____

ARE YOU PRE-QUALIFIED?
☐ YES   ☐ NO
ARE YOU WORKING WITH AN AGENT?
☐ YES   ☐ NO

NAME: _____

EMAIL: _____

PHONE: _____

ARE YOU PRE-QUALIFIED?
☐ YES   ☐ NO
ARE YOU WORKING WITH AN AGENT?
☐ YES   ☐ NO

NAME: _____

EMAIL: _____

PHONE: _____

ARE YOU PRE-QUALIFIED?
☐ YES   ☐ NO
ARE YOU WORKING WITH AN AGENT?
☐ YES   ☐ NO

NAME: _____

EMAIL: _____

PHONE: _____

ARE YOU PRE-QUALIFIED?
☐ YES   ☐ NO
ARE YOU WORKING WITH AN AGENT?
☐ YES   ☐ NO

NAME: _____

EMAIL: _____

PHONE: _____

ARE YOU PRE-QUALIFIED?
☐ YES   ☐ NO
ARE YOU WORKING WITH AN AGENT?
☐ YES   ☐ NO

Daily Ritual

DATE

MORNING PUMP UP	
MORNING MEDITATION	**READ 10 - 15 MIN**

AFFIRMATIONS
1
2
3

TOP THREE		

SCHEDULE			CALLS TO MAKE
			EMAILS TO WRITE
			NOTES

Seller Profile

CLIENT 1 - MR / MRS		
ADDRESS	**PHONE #**	
	EMAIL	

CLIENT 2 - MR / MRS		
ADDRESS	**PHONE #**	
	EMAIL	

LISTING DETAILS		
LISTING APPOINTMENT ☐	☐	☐
SUGGESTED LISTING PRICE RANGE		
BEDROOMS	**BATHS**	**SQUARE FOOTAGE**
DETAILS		
MORTGAGE BALANCE		**INTEREST RATE**
LIENS		**HOA FEES**

TITLE COMPANY		
NAME		
COMPANY		
PHONE	**FAX**	**EMAIL**

COOPERATING AGENT		
NAME		
COMPANY		
PHONE	**FAX**	**EMAIL**

NOTES

Prospecting Contacts

NAME			PHONE NUMBER #
BUYER	SELLER	OTHER	PHONE NUMBER #
ADDRESS			APPOINTMENT INFO
			FOLLOW UP
NOTES			

NAME			PHONE NUMBER #
BUYER	SELLER	OTHER	PHONE NUMBER #
			APPOINTMENT INFO
			FOLLOW UP
NOTES			

NAME			PHONE NUMBER #
BUYER	SELLER	OTHER	PHONE NUMBER #
			APPOINTMENT INFO
			FOLLOW UP
NOTES			

NAME			PHONE NUMBER #
BUYER	SELLER	OTHER	PHONE NUMBER #
			APPOINTMENT INFO
			FOLLOW UP
NOTES			

Vision Board

"Without execution, vision is just another word for hallucination." - Mark Hurd

Prospecting Worksheet

DATE

START TIME   END TIME

CALL TRACKING

| X CONTACT MADE | 0 PROSPECT FOLLOW UP | ✔ APPT. SCHEDULED |

CONTACTS

NAME	PHONE NUMBER #
BUYER SELLER OTHER	PHONE NUMBER #
ADDRESS	APPOINTMENT INFO
	FOLLOW UP
NOTES	

NAME	PHONE NUMBER #
BUYER SELLER OTHER	PHONE NUMBER #
	APPOINTMENT INFO
	FOLLOW UP
NOTES	

NAME	PHONE NUMBER #
BUYER SELLER OTHER	PHONE NUMBER #
	APPOINTMENT INFO
	FOLLOW UP
NOTES	

Goal Planning 2019

"A goal is a dream with a deadline" - Napoleon Hill

GOAL:

WHY IT'S MEANINGFUL:

HOW:

MONTHLY STEPS:

- ○
- ○
- ○
- ○
- ○
- ○

- ○
- ○
- ○
- ○
- ○
- ○

DAILY STEPS:

_____

_____

_____

_____

Goal Planning 2019

"Happiness is not a goal...it's a by-product of a life well lived." - Eleanor Roosevelt

	NUMBER OF CLOSINGS	AVG COMMISSION PER CLOSING
FIRST 6 MONTHS		
LAST 6 MONTHS		

PROSPECTING GOALS

MARKETING GOALS

NETWORKING GOALS

PROFESSIONAL DEVELOPMENT GOALS

MONTH OF: January 2019

Goal Planning 2019

MONTHLY GOALS:

_____

_____

_____

_____

1 2 3 4 5

WEEKLY GOALS:

_____

_____

_____

_____

_____

_____

_____

WHAT WORKED THIS MONTH

_____

_____

_____

_____

_____

_____

_____

_____

_____

WHAT HAS NOT WORKED THIS MONTH

_____

_____

_____

_____

_____

_____

_____

_____

_____

Closings Tracker

NAME	ADDRESS	DATE	AMOUNT

Buyer Profile

CLIENT 1 - MR / MRS	
ADDRESS	**PHONE #**
	EMAIL
CLIENT 2 - MR / MRS	
ADDRESS	**PHONE #**
	EMAIL

DETAILS

PRICE RANGE	**BEDROOMS**	**BATHS**
AREAS		
MUST HAVES		
PREAPPROVED? YES	**NO** **AMOUNT**	
HOW THEY HEARD ABOUT ME		
CONTACT DATE	**FOLLOW UP DATE**	
CONTACT DATE	**FOLLOW UP DATE**	

LENDER CONTACT

NAME		
COMPANY		
PHONE	**FAX**	**EMAIL**

TITLE COMPANY

NAME		
COMPANY		
PHONE	**FAX**	**EMAIL**

COOPERATING AGENT

NAME		
COMPANY		
PHONE	**FAX**	**EMAIL**

Backward Goal Setting

Work backwards from your ultimate goal and figure out what you need to get you there.

GOAL FOR SOMEDAY:
What's your ulitmate goal?

FIVE - YEAR GOAL:
based on your goal above, what can you do in the next five years to get you closer to your goal?

ONE - YEAR GOAL:
based on your goal above, what can you do in the next year to get you closer to your goal?

MONTHLY GOAL:
based on your goal above, what can you do in the next month to get you closer to your goal?

WEEKLY GOAL:
based on your goal above, what can you do in the next week to get you closer to your goal?

DAILY GOAL:
based on your goal above, what can you do today to get you closer to your goal?

GOAL FOR RIGHT NOW:
based on your goal above, what can you do right now?

DELISHA BOYD LLC

Event Sign In Sheet

NAME: _____

EMAIL: _____

PHONE: _____

ARE YOU PRE-QUALIFIED?

☐ YES ☐ NO

ARE YOU WORKING WITH AN AGENT?

☐ YES ☐ NO

NAME: _____

EMAIL: _____

PHONE: _____

ARE YOU PRE-QUALIFIED?

☐ YES ☐ NO

ARE YOU WORKING WITH AN AGENT?

☐ YES ☐ NO

NAME: _____

EMAIL: _____

PHONE: _____

ARE YOU PRE-QUALIFIED?

☐ YES ☐ NO

ARE YOU WORKING WITH AN AGENT?

☐ YES ☐ NO

NAME: _____

EMAIL: _____

PHONE: _____

ARE YOU PRE-QUALIFIED?

☐ YES ☐ NO

ARE YOU WORKING WITH AN AGENT?

☐ YES ☐ NO

NAME: _____

EMAIL: _____

PHONE: _____

ARE YOU PRE-QUALIFIED?

☐ YES ☐ NO

ARE YOU WORKING WITH AN AGENT?

☐ YES ☐ NO

NAME: _____

EMAIL: _____

PHONE: _____

ARE YOU PRE-QUALIFIED?

☐ YES ☐ NO

ARE YOU WORKING WITH AN AGENT?

☐ YES ☐ NO

NAME: _____

EMAIL: _____

PHONE: _____

ARE YOU PRE-QUALIFIED?

☐ YES ☐ NO

ARE YOU WORKING WITH AN AGENT?

☐ YES ☐ NO

Daily Ritual

DATE

MORNING PUMP UP	
MORNING MEDITATION	READ 10 - 15 MIN

AFFIRMATIONS	
1	
2	
3	

TOP THREE		

SCHEDULE		CALLS TO MAKE
		EMAILS TO WRITE
		NOTES

Seller Profile

CLIENT 1 - MR / MRS	
ADDRESS	**PHONE #**
	EMAIL

CLIENT 2 - MR / MRS	
ADDRESS	**PHONE #**
	EMAIL

LISTING DETAILS

LISTING APPOINTMENT ☐	☐	☐
SUGGESTED LISTING PRICE RANGE		
BEDROOMS	**BATHS**	**SQUARE FOOTAGE**
DETAILS		
MORTGAGE BALANCE		**INTEREST RATE**
LIENS		**HOA FEES**

TITLE COMPANY

NAME		
COMPANY		
PHONE	**FAX**	**EMAIL**

COOPERATING AGENT

NAME		
COMPANY		
PHONE	**FAX**	**EMAIL**

NOTES

Prospecting Contacts

NAME	PHONE NUMBER #
BUYER SELLER OTHER	PHONE NUMBER #
ADDRESS	APPOINTMENT INFO
	FOLLOW UP
NOTES	

NAME	PHONE NUMBER #
BUYER SELLER OTHER	PHONE NUMBER #
	APPOINTMENT INFO
	FOLLOW UP
NOTES	

NAME	PHONE NUMBER #
BUYER SELLER OTHER	PHONE NUMBER #
	APPOINTMENT INFO
	FOLLOW UP
NOTES	

NAME	PHONE NUMBER #
BUYER SELLER OTHER	PHONE NUMBER #
	APPOINTMENT INFO
	FOLLOW UP
NOTES	

Vision Board

"The Vision should be followed by an action. You can't stare at the stairs, you have to take the first step" Delisha Young Boyd

Prospecting Worksheet

DATE

START TIME   **END TIME**

CALL TRACKING

X CONTACT MADE	O PROSPECT FOLLOW UP	✔ APPT. SCHEDULED

CONTACTS

NAME	PHONE NUMBER #
BUYER SELLER OTHER	PHONE NUMBER #
ADDRESS	APPOINTMENT INFO
	FOLLOW UP
NOTES	

NAME	PHONE NUMBER #
BUYER SELLER OTHER	PHONE NUMBER #
	APPOINTMENT INFO
	FOLLOW UP
NOTES	

NAME	PHONE NUMBER #
BUYER SELLER OTHER	PHONE NUMBER #
	APPOINTMENT INFO
	FOLLOW UP
NOTES	

Goal Planning 2019

"I don't focus on what I'm up against. I focus on my goals and I try to ignore the rest." - Venus Williams

GOAL:

WHY IT'S MEANINGFUL:

HOW:

MONTHLY STEPS:

- ◯
- ◯
- ◯
- ◯
- ◯
- ◯

- ◯
- ◯
- ◯
- ◯
- ◯
- ◯

DAILY STEPS:

_____   _____

_____   _____

_____   _____

Goal Planning 2019

"Your goals are the road maps that guide you and show you what's possible in your life." - Les Brown

	NUMBER OF CLOSINGS	AVG COMMISSION PER CLOSING
FIRST 6 MONTHS		
LAST 6 MONTHS		

PROSPECTING GOALS

MARKETING GOALS

NETWORKING GOALS

PROFESSIONAL DEVELOPMENT GOALS

MONTH OF: February 2019

Goal Planning 2019

MONTHLY GOALS:

_____

_____

_____

_____

1   2   3   4   5

WEEKLY GOALS:

_____

_____

_____

_____

_____

_____

_____

WHAT WORKED THIS MONTH

_____

_____

_____

_____

_____

_____

_____

_____

WHAT HAS NOT WORKED THIS MONTH

_____

_____

_____

_____

_____

_____

_____

_____

Closings Tracker

NAME	ADDRESS	DATE	AMOUNT

Buyer Profile

CLIENT 1 - MR / MRS	
ADDRESS	**PHONE #**
	EMAIL

CLIENT 2 - MR / MRS	
ADDRESS	**PHONE #**
	EMAIL

DETAILS

PRICE RANGE	**BEDROOMS**	**BATHS**
AREAS		
MUST HAVES		
PREAPPROVED? YES NO **AMOUNT**		
HOW THEY HEARD ABOUT ME		
CONTACT DATE	**FOLLOW UP DATE**	
CONTACT DATE	**FOLLOW UP DATE**	

LENDER CONTACT

NAME		
COMPANY		
PHONE	**FAX**	**EMAIL**

TITLE COMPANY

NAME		
COMPANY		
PHONE	**FAX**	**EMAIL**

COOPERATING AGENT

NAME		
COMPANY		
PHONE	**FAX**	**EMAIL**

Backward Goal Setting

Work backwards from your ultimate goal and figure out what you need to get you there.

GOAL FOR SOMEDAY:
What's your ulitmate goal?

FIVE - YEAR GOAL:
based on your goal above, what can you do in the next five years to get you closer to your goal?

ONE - YEAR GOAL:
based on your goal above, what can you do in the next year to get you closer to your goal?

MONTHLY GOAL:
based on your goal above, what can you do in the next month to get you closer to your goal?

WEEKLY GOAL:
based on your goal above, what can you do in the next week to get you closer to your goal?

DAILY GOAL:
based on your goal above, what can you do today to get you closer to your goal?

GOAL FOR RIGHT NOW:
based on your goal above, what can you do right now?

DELISHA BOYD LLC

Event Sign In Sheet

NAME: _____

EMAIL: _____

PHONE: _____

ARE YOU PRE-QUALIFIED?
☐ YES ☐ NO
ARE YOU WORKING WITH AN AGENT?
☐ YES ☐ NO

NAME: _____

EMAIL: _____

PHONE: _____

ARE YOU PRE-QUALIFIED?
☐ YES ☐ NO
ARE YOU WORKING WITH AN AGENT?
☐ YES ☐ NO

NAME: _____

EMAIL: _____

PHONE: _____

ARE YOU PRE-QUALIFIED?
☐ YES ☐ NO
ARE YOU WORKING WITH AN AGENT?
☐ YES ☐ NO

NAME: _____

EMAIL: _____

PHONE: _____

ARE YOU PRE-QUALIFIED?
☐ YES ☐ NO
ARE YOU WORKING WITH AN AGENT?
☐ YES ☐ NO

NAME: _____

EMAIL: _____

PHONE: _____

ARE YOU PRE-QUALIFIED?
☐ YES ☐ NO
ARE YOU WORKING WITH AN AGENT?
☐ YES ☐ NO

NAME: _____

EMAIL: _____

PHONE: _____

ARE YOU PRE-QUALIFIED?
☐ YES ☐ NO
ARE YOU WORKING WITH AN AGENT?
☐ YES ☐ NO

NAME: _____

EMAIL: _____

PHONE: _____

ARE YOU PRE-QUALIFIED?
☐ YES ☐ NO
ARE YOU WORKING WITH AN AGENT?
☐ YES ☐ NO

Daily Ritual

DATE

MORNING PUMP UP	
MORNING MEDITATION	READ 10 - 15 MIN

AFFIRMATIONS	
1	
2	
3	

TOP THREE		

SCHEDULE			CALLS TO MAKE
			EMAILS TO WRITE
			NOTES

Seller Profile

CLIENT 1 - MR / MRS	
ADDRESS	**PHONE #**
	EMAIL
CLIENT 2 - MR / MRS	
ADDRESS	**PHONE #**
	EMAIL

LISTING DETAILS

LISTING APPOINTMENT ☐	☐	☐
SUGGESTED LISTING PRICE RANGE		
BEDROOMS	**BATHS**	**SQUARE FOOTAGE**
DETAILS		
MORTGAGE BALANCE		**INTEREST RATE**
LIENS		**HOA FEES**

TITLE COMPANY

NAME		
COMPANY		
PHONE	**FAX**	**EMAIL**

COOPERATING AGENT

NAME		
COMPANY		
PHONE	**FAX**	**EMAIL**

NOTES

Prospecting Contacts

NAME	PHONE NUMBER #
BUYER SELLER OTHER	PHONE NUMBER #
ADDRESS	APPOINTMENT INFO
	FOLLOW UP
NOTES	

NAME	PHONE NUMBER #
BUYER SELLER OTHER	PHONE NUMBER #
	APPOINTMENT INFO
	FOLLOW UP
NOTES	

NAME	PHONE NUMBER #
BUYER SELLER OTHER	PHONE NUMBER #
	APPOINTMENT INFO
	FOLLOW UP
NOTES	

NAME	PHONE NUMBER #
BUYER SELLER OTHER	PHONE NUMBER #
	APPOINTMENT INFO
	FOLLOW UP
NOTES	

Vision Board

"Create the highest grandest vision possible for your life, because you become what you believe." Oprah Winfrey

Prospecting Worksheet

CALL TRACKING

X	CONTACT MADE	0	PROSPECT FOLLOW UP	✔	APPT. SCHEDULED

CONTACTS

NAME	PHONE NUMBER #
BUYER SELLER OTHER	PHONE NUMBER #
ADDRESS	APPOINTMENT INFO
	FOLLOW UP
NOTES	

NAME	PHONE NUMBER #
BUYER SELLER OTHER	PHONE NUMBER #
	APPOINTMENT INFO
	FOLLOW UP
NOTES	

NAME	PHONE NUMBER #
BUYER SELLER OTHER	PHONE NUMBER #
	APPOINTMENT INFO
	FOLLOW UP
NOTES	

Goal Planning 2019

"Setting goals is the first step in turning the invisible into the visible." - Tony Robbins

GOAL:

WHY IT'S MEANINGFUL:

HOW:

MONTHLY STEPS:

- ○
- ○
- ○
- ○
- ○
- ○

- ○
- ○
- ○
- ○
- ○
- ○

DAILY STEPS:

_____

_____

_____

_____

Goal Planning 2019

"People with goals succeed because they know where they're going"
Earl Nightingale

	NUMBER OF CLOSINGS	AVG COMMISSION PER CLOSING
FIRST 6 MONTHS		
LAST 6 MONTHS		

PROSPECTING GOALS

MARKETING GOALS

NETWORKING GOALS

PROFESSIONAL DEVELOPMENT GOALS

MONTH OF: March 2019

Goal Planning 2019

MONTHLY GOALS:

_____

_____

_____

_____

1 2 3 4 5

WEEKLY GOALS:

_____

_____

_____

_____

_____

_____

WHAT WORKED THIS MONTH

_____

_____

_____

_____

_____

_____

_____

WHAT HAS NOT WORKED THIS MONTH

_____

_____

_____

_____

_____

_____

_____

Closings Tracker

NAME	ADDRESS	DATE	AMOUNT

Buyer Profile

CLIENT 1 - MR / MRS		
ADDRESS	PHONE #	
	EMAIL	

CLIENT 2 - MR / MRS		
ADDRESS	PHONE #	
	EMAIL	

DETAILS

PRICE RANGE	BEDROOMS	BATHS
AREAS		
MUST HAVES		
PREAPPROVED? YES	NO AMOUNT	
HOW THEY HEARD ABOUT ME		
CONTACT DATE	FOLLOW UP DATE	
CONTACT DATE	FOLLOW UP DATE	

LENDER CONTACT

NAME		
COMPANY		
PHONE	FAX	EMAIL

TITLE COMPANY

NAME		
COMPANY		
PHONE	FAX	EMAIL

COOPERATING AGENT

NAME		
COMPANY		
PHONE	FAX	EMAIL

Backward Goal Setting

Work backwards from your ultimate goal and figure out what you need to get you there.

GOAL FOR SOMEDAY:
What's your ulitmate goal?

FIVE - YEAR GOAL:
based on your goal above, what can you do in the next five years to get you closer to your goal?

ONE - YEAR GOAL:
based on your goal above, what can you do in the next year to get you closer to your goal?

MONTHLY GOAL:
based on your goal above, what can you do in the next month to get you closer to your goal?

WEEKLY GOAL:
based on your goal above, what can you do in the next week to get you closer to your goal?

DAILY GOAL:
based on your goal above, what can you do today to get you closer to your goal?

GOAL FOR RIGHT NOW:
based on your goal above, what can you do right now?

Event Sign In Sheet

NAME: _____

EMAIL: _____

PHONE: _____

ARE YOU PRE-QUALIFIED?
☐ YES   ☐ NO
ARE YOU WORKING WITH AN AGENT?
☐ YES   ☐ NO

NAME: _____

EMAIL: _____

PHONE: _____

ARE YOU PRE-QUALIFIED?
☐ YES   ☐ NO
ARE YOU WORKING WITH AN AGENT?
☐ YES   ☐ NO

NAME: _____

EMAIL: _____

PHONE: _____

ARE YOU PRE-QUALIFIED?
☐ YES   ☐ NO
ARE YOU WORKING WITH AN AGENT?
☐ YES   ☐ NO

NAME: _____

EMAIL: _____

PHONE: _____

ARE YOU PRE-QUALIFIED?
☐ YES   ☐ NO
ARE YOU WORKING WITH AN AGENT?
☐ YES   ☐ NO

NAME: _____

EMAIL: _____

PHONE: _____

ARE YOU PRE-QUALIFIED?
☐ YES   ☐ NO
ARE YOU WORKING WITH AN AGENT?
☐ YES   ☐ NO

NAME: _____

EMAIL: _____

PHONE: _____

ARE YOU PRE-QUALIFIED?
☐ YES   ☐ NO
ARE YOU WORKING WITH AN AGENT?
☐ YES   ☐ NO

NAME: _____

EMAIL: _____

PHONE: _____

ARE YOU PRE-QUALIFIED?
☐ YES   ☐ NO
ARE YOU WORKING WITH AN AGENT?
☐ YES   ☐ NO

Daily Ritual

DATE

MORNING PUMP UP	
MORNING MEDITATION	READ 10 - 15 MIN

AFFIRMATIONS
1
2
3

TOP THREE		

SCHEDULE			CALLS TO MAKE
			EMAILS TO WRITE
			NOTES

Seller Profile

CLIENT 1 - MR / MRS	
ADDRESS	**PHONE #**
	EMAIL
CLIENT 2 - MR / MRS	
ADDRESS	**PHONE #**
	EMAIL

LISTING DETAILS

LISTING APPOINTMENT ☐	☐	☐
SUGGESTED LISTING PRICE RANGE		
BEDROOMS	**BATHS**	**SQUARE FOOTAGE**
DETAILS		
MORTGAGE BALANCE		**INTEREST RATE**
LIENS		**HOA FEES**

TITLE COMPANY

NAME		
COMPANY		
PHONE	**FAX**	**EMAIL**

COOPERATING AGENT

NAME		
COMPANY		
PHONE	**FAX**	**EMAIL**

NOTES

Prospecting Contacts

NAME			PHONE NUMBER #
BUYER	SELLER	OTHER	PHONE NUMBER #
ADDRESS			APPOINTMENT INFO
			FOLLOW UP
NOTES			

NAME			PHONE NUMBER #
BUYER	SELLER	OTHER	PHONE NUMBER #
			APPOINTMENT INFO
			FOLLOW UP
NOTES			

NAME			PHONE NUMBER #
BUYER	SELLER	OTHER	PHONE NUMBER #
			APPOINTMENT INFO
			FOLLOW UP
NOTES			

NAME			PHONE NUMBER #
BUYER	SELLER	OTHER	PHONE NUMBER #
			APPOINTMENT INFO
			FOLLOW UP
NOTES			

Vision Board

"A leader has the vision and conviction that a dream can be achieved. He inspires the power and energy to get it done." – Ralph Lauren

Prospecting Worksheet

CALL TRACKING

X CONTACT MADE	0 PROSPECT FOLLOW UP	✔ APPT. SCHEDULED

CONTACTS

NAME	PHONE NUMBER #
BUYER SELLER OTHER	PHONE NUMBER #
ADDRESS	APPOINTMENT INFO
	FOLLOW UP
NOTES	

NAME	PHONE NUMBER #
BUYER SELLER OTHER	PHONE NUMBER #
	APPOINTMENT INFO
	FOLLOW UP
NOTES	

NAME	PHONE NUMBER #
BUYER SELLER OTHER	PHONE NUMBER #
	APPOINTMENT INFO
	FOLLOW UP
NOTES	

Goal Planning 2019

"Goals are the fuel in the furnace of achievement."- Brian Tracy

GOAL:

WHY IT'S MEANINGFUL:

HOW:

MONTHLY STEPS:

- ○
- ○
- ○
- ○
- ○
- ○

- ○
- ○
- ○
- ○
- ○
- ○

DAILY STEPS:

_____

_____

_____

_____

Goal Planning 2019

"Review your goals twice every day in order to be focused on achieving them" - Les Brown

	NUMBER OF CLOSINGS	AVG COMMISSION PER CLOSING
FIRST 6 MONTHS		
LAST 6 MONTHS		

PROSPECTING GOALS

MARKETING GOALS

NETWORKING GOALS

PROFESSIONAL DEVELOPMENT GOALS

MONTH OF: April 2019

Goal Planning 2019

MONTHLY GOALS:

_____
_____
_____
_____

1 2 3 4 5

WEEKLY GOALS:

_____
_____
_____
_____
_____
_____

WHAT WORKED THIS MONTH

_____
_____
_____
_____
_____
_____
_____
_____
_____
_____

WHAT HAS NOT WORKED THIS MONTH

_____
_____
_____
_____
_____
_____
_____
_____
_____
_____

Closings Tracker

NAME	ADDRESS	DATE	AMOUNT

Buyer Profile

CLIENT 1 - MR / MRS	
ADDRESS	**PHONE #**
	EMAIL

CLIENT 2 - MR / MRS	
ADDRESS	**PHONE #**
	EMAIL

DETAILS

PRICE RANGE	**BEDROOMS**	**BATHS**
AREAS		
MUST HAVES		
PREAPPROVED? YES NO **AMOUNT**		
HOW THEY HEARD ABOUT ME		
CONTACT DATE	**FOLLOW UP DATE**	
CONTACT DATE	**FOLLOW UP DATE**	

LENDER CONTACT

NAME		
COMPANY		
PHONE	**FAX**	**EMAIL**

TITLE COMPANY

NAME		
COMPANY		
PHONE	**FAX**	**EMAIL**

COOPERATING AGENT

NAME		
COMPANY		
PHONE	**FAX**	**EMAIL**

Backward Goal Setting

Work backwards from your ultimate goal and figure out what you need to get you there.

GOAL FOR SOMEDAY:
What's your ulitmate goal?

FIVE - YEAR GOAL:
based on your goal above, what can you do in the next five years to get you closer to your goal?

ONE - YEAR GOAL:
based on your goal above, what can you do in the next year to get you closer to your goal?

MONTHLY GOAL:
based on your goal above, what can you do in the next month to get you closer to your goal?

WEEKLY GOAL:
based on your goal above, what can you do in the next week to get you closer to your goal?

DAILY GOAL:
based on your goal above, what can you do today to get you closer to your goal?

GOAL FOR RIGHT NOW:
based on your goal above, what can you do right now?

DELISHA BOYD LLC

Event Sign In Sheet

NAME: _____

EMAIL: _____

PHONE: _____

ARE YOU PRE-QUALIFIED?
☐ YES   ☐ NO
ARE YOU WORKING WITH AN AGENT?
☐ YES   ☐ NO

NAME: _____

EMAIL: _____

PHONE: _____

ARE YOU PRE-QUALIFIED?
☐ YES   ☐ NO
ARE YOU WORKING WITH AN AGENT?
☐ YES   ☐ NO

NAME: _____

EMAIL: _____

PHONE: _____

ARE YOU PRE-QUALIFIED?
☐ YES   ☐ NO
ARE YOU WORKING WITH AN AGENT?
☐ YES   ☐ NO

NAME: _____

EMAIL: _____

PHONE: _____

ARE YOU PRE-QUALIFIED?
☐ YES   ☐ NO
ARE YOU WORKING WITH AN AGENT?
☐ YES   ☐ NO

NAME: _____

EMAIL: _____

PHONE: _____

ARE YOU PRE-QUALIFIED?
☐ YES   ☐ NO
ARE YOU WORKING WITH AN AGENT?
☐ YES   ☐ NO

NAME: _____

EMAIL: _____

PHONE: _____

ARE YOU PRE-QUALIFIED?
☐ YES   ☐ NO
ARE YOU WORKING WITH AN AGENT?
☐ YES   ☐ NO

NAME: _____

EMAIL: _____

PHONE: _____

ARE YOU PRE-QUALIFIED?
☐ YES   ☐ NO
ARE YOU WORKING WITH AN AGENT?
☐ YES   ☐ NO

Daily Ritual

DATE

MORNING PUMP UP	
MORNING MEDITATION	**READ 10 - 15 MIN**

AFFIRMATIONS
1
2
3

TOP THREE		

SCHEDULE			CALLS TO MAKE
			EMAILS TO WRITE
			NOTES

Seller Profile

CLIENT 1 - MR / MRS	
ADDRESS	**PHONE #**
	EMAIL
CLIENT 2 - MR / MRS	
ADDRESS	**PHONE #**
	EMAIL

LISTING DETAILS		
LISTING APPOINTMENT ☐	☐	☐
SUGGESTED LISTING PRICE RANGE		
BEDROOMS	**BATHS**	**SQUARE FOOTAGE**
DETAILS		
MORTGAGE BALANCE		**INTEREST RATE**
LIENS		**HOA FEES**

TITLE COMPANY		
NAME		
COMPANY		
PHONE	**FAX**	**EMAIL**

COOPERATING AGENT		
NAME		
COMPANY		
PHONE	**FAX**	**EMAIL**

NOTES

Prospecting Contacts

NAME			PHONE NUMBER #
BUYER	SELLER	OTHER	PHONE NUMBER #
ADDRESS			APPOINTMENT INFO
			FOLLOW UP
NOTES			

NAME			PHONE NUMBER #
BUYER	SELLER	OTHER	PHONE NUMBER #
			APPOINTMENT INFO
			FOLLOW UP
NOTES			

NAME			PHONE NUMBER #
BUYER	SELLER	OTHER	PHONE NUMBER #
			APPOINTMENT INFO
			FOLLOW UP
NOTES			

NAME			PHONE NUMBER #
BUYER	SELLER	OTHER	PHONE NUMBER #
			APPOINTMENT INFO
			FOLLOW UP
NOTES			

Vision Board

"The vision that you glorify in your mind, the ideal that you enthrone in your heart, this you will build your life by, and this you will become."
– Anonymous

Prospecting Worksheet

DATE

START TIME   **END TIME**

CALL TRACKING

X	CONTACT MADE	0	PROSPECT FOLLOW UP	✔	APPT. SCHEDULED

☐ ☐ ☐ ☐ ☐ ☐ ☐ ☐ ☐ ☐ ☐ ☐ ☐ ☐ ☐ ☐

☐ ☐ ☐ ☐ ☐ ☐ ☐ ☐ ☐ ☐ ☐ ☐ ☐ ☐ ☐ ☐

☐ ☐ ☐ ☐ ☐ ☐ ☐ ☐ ☐ ☐ ☐ ☐ ☐ ☐ ☐ ☐

☐ ☐ ☐ ☐ ☐ ☐ ☐ ☐ ☐ ☐ ☐ ☐ ☐ ☐ ☐ ☐

CONTACTS

NAME			PHONE NUMBER #
BUYER	SELLER	OTHER	PHONE NUMBER #
ADDRESS			APPOINTMENT INFO
			FOLLOW UP
NOTES			

NAME			PHONE NUMBER #
BUYER	SELLER	OTHER	PHONE NUMBER #
			APPOINTMENT INFO
			FOLLOW UP
NOTES			

NAME			PHONE NUMBER #
BUYER	SELLER	OTHER	PHONE NUMBER #
			APPOINTMENT INFO
			FOLLOW UP
NOTES			

Goal Planning 2019

"Think little goals and expect little achievements. Think big goals and win big success."
David Joseph Schwartz

GOAL:

WHY IT'S MEANINGFUL:

HOW:

MONTHLY STEPS:

○
○
○
○
○
○

○
○
○
○
○
○

DAILY STEPS:

_____

_____

_____

_____

_____

_____

_____

_____

Goal Planning 2019

"Your goals, minus your doubts, equal your reality" - Ralph Marston

	NUMBER OF CLOSINGS	AVG COMMISSION PER CLOSING
FIRST 6 MONTHS		
LAST 6 MONTHS		

PROSPECTING GOALS

MARKETING GOALS

NETWORKING GOALS

PROFESSIONAL DEVELOPMENT GOALS

MONTH OF: May 2019

Goal Planning 2019

MONTHLY GOALS:

_____

_____

_____

_____

1 2 3 4 5

WEEKLY GOALS:

_____

_____

_____

_____

_____

_____

WHAT WORKED THIS MONTH

_____

_____

_____

_____

_____

_____

_____

_____

WHAT HAS NOT WORKED THIS MONTH

_____

_____

_____

_____

_____

_____

_____

_____

Closings Tracker

NAME	ADDRESS	DATE	AMOUNT

Buyer Profile

CLIENT 1 - MR / MRS	
ADDRESS	**PHONE #**
	EMAIL
CLIENT 2 - MR / MRS	
ADDRESS	**PHONE #**
	EMAIL

DETAILS

PRICE RANGE	**BEDROOMS**	**BATHS**
AREAS		
MUST HAVES		
PREAPPROVED? YES NO **AMOUNT**		
HOW THEY HEARD ABOUT ME		
CONTACT DATE	**FOLLOW UP DATE**	
CONTACT DATE	**FOLLOW UP DATE**	

LENDER CONTACT

NAME		
COMPANY		
PHONE	**FAX**	**EMAIL**

TITLE COMPANY

NAME		
COMPANY		
PHONE	**FAX**	**EMAIL**

COOPERATING AGENT

NAME		
COMPANY		
PHONE	**FAX**	**EMAIL**

Backward Goal Setting

Work backwards from your ultimate goal and figure out what you need to get you there.

GOAL FOR SOMEDAY:
What's your ulitmate goal?

FIVE - YEAR GOAL:
based on your goal above, what can you do in the next five years to get you closer to your goal?

ONE - YEAR GOAL:
based on your goal above, what can you do in the next year to get you closer to your goal?

MONTHLY GOAL:
based on your goal above, what can you do in the next month to get you closer to your goal?

WEEKLY GOAL:
based on your goal above, what can you do in the next week to get you closer to your goal?

DAILY GOAL:
based on your goal above, what can you do today to get you closer to your goal?

GOAL FOR RIGHT NOW:
based on your goal above, what can you do right now?

Event Sign In Sheet

NAME: _____

EMAIL: _____

PHONE: _____

ARE YOU PRE-QUALIFIED?

YES ☐   NO ☐

ARE YOU WORKING WITH AN AGENT?

YES ☐   NO ☐

NAME: _____

EMAIL: _____

PHONE: _____

ARE YOU PRE-QUALIFIED?

YES ☐   NO ☐

ARE YOU WORKING WITH AN AGENT?

YES ☐   NO ☐

NAME: _____

EMAIL: _____

PHONE: _____

ARE YOU PRE-QUALIFIED?

YES ☐   NO ☐

ARE YOU WORKING WITH AN AGENT?

YES ☐   NO ☐

NAME: _____

EMAIL: _____

PHONE: _____

ARE YOU PRE-QUALIFIED?

YES ☐   NO ☐

ARE YOU WORKING WITH AN AGENT?

YES ☐   NO ☐

NAME: _____

EMAIL: _____

PHONE: _____

ARE YOU PRE-QUALIFIED?

YES ☐   NO ☐

ARE YOU WORKING WITH AN AGENT?

YES ☐   NO ☐

NAME: _____

EMAIL: _____

PHONE: _____

ARE YOU PRE-QUALIFIED?

YES ☐   NO ☐

ARE YOU WORKING WITH AN AGENT?

YES ☐   NO ☐

NAME: _____

EMAIL: _____

PHONE: _____

ARE YOU PRE-QUALIFIED?

YES ☐   NO ☐

ARE YOU WORKING WITH AN AGENT?

YES ☐   NO ☐

Daily Ritual

DATE

MORNING PUMP UP	
MORNING MEDITATION	READ 10 - 15 MIN

AFFIRMATIONS	
1	
2	
3	

TOP THREE		

SCHEDULE			CALLS TO MAKE
			EMAILS TO WRITE
			NOTES

Seller Profile

CLIENT 1 - MR / MRS	
ADDRESS	**PHONE #**
	EMAIL

CLIENT 2 - MR / MRS	
ADDRESS	**PHONE #**
	EMAIL

LISTING DETAILS

LISTING APPOINTMENT	☐	☐	☐
SUGGESTED LISTING PRICE RANGE			
BEDROOMS	**BATHS**	**SQUARE FOOTAGE**	
DETAILS			
MORTGAGE BALANCE		**INTEREST RATE**	
LIENS		**HOA FEES**	

TITLE COMPANY

NAME		
COMPANY		
PHONE	**FAX**	**EMAIL**

COOPERATING AGENT

NAME		
COMPANY		
PHONE	**FAX**	**EMAIL**

NOTES

Prospecting Contacts

NAME			PHONE NUMBER #
BUYER	SELLER	OTHER	PHONE NUMBER #
ADDRESS			APPOINTMENT INFO
			FOLLOW UP
NOTES			

NAME			PHONE NUMBER #
BUYER	SELLER	OTHER	PHONE NUMBER #
			APPOINTMENT INFO
			FOLLOW UP
NOTES			

NAME			PHONE NUMBER #
BUYER	SELLER	OTHER	PHONE NUMBER #
			APPOINTMENT INFO
			FOLLOW UP
NOTES			

NAME			PHONE NUMBER #
BUYER	SELLER	OTHER	PHONE NUMBER #
			APPOINTMENT INFO
			FOLLOW UP
NOTES			

Vision Board

"Where there is no vision the people perish." - Proverbs 29:18

Prospecting Worksheet

DATE

START TIME   END TIME

CALL TRACKING		

X CONTACT MADE	O PROSPECT FOLLOW UP	✓ APPT. SCHEDULED

CONTACTS

NAME	PHONE NUMBER #
BUYER SELLER OTHER	PHONE NUMBER #
ADDRESS	APPOINTMENT INFO
	FOLLOW UP
NOTES	

NAME	PHONE NUMBER #
BUYER SELLER OTHER	PHONE NUMBER #
	APPOINTMENT INFO
	FOLLOW UP
NOTES	

NAME	PHONE NUMBER #
BUYER SELLER OTHER	PHONE NUMBER #
	APPOINTMENT INFO
	FOLLOW UP
NOTES	

Goal Planning 2019

"A goal properly set is halfway reached." – Zig Ziglar

GOAL:

WHY IT'S MEANINGFUL:

HOW:

MONTHLY STEPS:

- ○
- ○
- ○
- ○
- ○
- ○

- ○
- ○
- ○
- ○
- ○
- ○

DAILY STEPS:

_____

_____

_____

_____

_____

_____

Goal Planning 2019

"Happiness is not a goal...it's a by-product of a life well lived." - Eleanor Roosevelt

	NUMBER OF CLOSINGS	AVG COMMISSION PER CLOSING
FIRST 6 MONTHS		
LAST 6 MONTHS		

PROSPECTING GOALS

MARKETING GOALS

NETWORKING GOALS

PROFESSIONAL DEVELOPMENT GOALS

MONTH OF: June 2019

Goal Planning 2019

MONTHLY GOALS:

_____

_____

_____

_____

1 2 3 4 5

WEEKLY GOALS:

_____

_____

_____

_____

_____

_____

_____

WHAT WORKED THIS MONTH

_____

_____

_____

_____

_____

_____

_____

_____

_____

WHAT HAS NOT WORKED THIS MONTH

_____

_____

_____

_____

_____

_____

_____

_____

_____

Closings Tracker

NAME	ADDRESS	DATE	AMOUNT

Buyer Profile

CLIENT 1 - MR / MRS	
ADDRESS	**PHONE #**
	EMAIL

CLIENT 2 - MR / MRS	
ADDRESS	**PHONE #**
	EMAIL

DETAILS

PRICE RANGE	**BEDROOMS**	**BATHS**
AREAS		
MUST HAVES		
PREAPPROVED? YES	NO **AMOUNT**	
HOW THEY HEARD ABOUT ME		
CONTACT DATE	**FOLLOW UP DATE**	
CONTACT DATE	**FOLLOW UP DATE**	

LENDER CONTACT

NAME		
COMPANY		
PHONE	**FAX**	**EMAIL**

TITLE COMPANY

NAME		
COMPANY		
PHONE	**FAX**	**EMAIL**

COOPERATING AGENT

NAME		
COMPANY		
PHONE	**FAX**	**EMAIL**

Backward Goal Setting

Work backwards from your ultimate goal and figure out what you need to get you there.

GOAL FOR SOMEDAY:
What's your ulitmate goal?

FIVE - YEAR GOAL:
based on your goal above, what can you do in the next five years to get you closer to your goal?

ONE - YEAR GOAL:
based on your goal above, what can you do in the next year to get you closer to your goal?

MONTHLY GOAL:
based on your goal above, what can you do in the next month to get you closer to your goal?

WEEKLY GOAL:
based on your goal above, what can you do in the next week to get you closer to your goal?

DAILY GOAL:
based on your goal above, what can you do today to get you closer to your goal?

GOAL FOR RIGHT NOW:
based on your goal above, what can you do right now?

DELISHA BOYD LLC

Event Sign In Sheet

NAME: _____

EMAIL: _____

PHONE: _____

ARE YOU PRE-QUALIFIED?
☐ YES ☐ NO
ARE YOU WORKING WITH AN AGENT?
☐ YES ☐ NO

NAME: _____

EMAIL: _____

PHONE: _____

ARE YOU PRE-QUALIFIED?
☐ YES ☐ NO
ARE YOU WORKING WITH AN AGENT?
☐ YES ☐ NO

NAME: _____

EMAIL: _____

PHONE: _____

ARE YOU PRE-QUALIFIED?
☐ YES ☐ NO
ARE YOU WORKING WITH AN AGENT?
☐ YES ☐ NO

NAME: _____

EMAIL: _____

PHONE: _____

ARE YOU PRE-QUALIFIED?
☐ YES ☐ NO
ARE YOU WORKING WITH AN AGENT?
☐ YES ☐ NO

NAME: _____

EMAIL: _____

PHONE: _____

ARE YOU PRE-QUALIFIED?
☐ YES ☐ NO
ARE YOU WORKING WITH AN AGENT?
☐ YES ☐ NO

NAME: _____

EMAIL: _____

PHONE: _____

ARE YOU PRE-QUALIFIED?
☐ YES ☐ NO
ARE YOU WORKING WITH AN AGENT?
☐ YES ☐ NO

NAME: _____

EMAIL: _____

PHONE: _____

ARE YOU PRE-QUALIFIED?
☐ YES ☐ NO
ARE YOU WORKING WITH AN AGENT?
☐ YES ☐ NO

Daily Ritual

DATE

MORNING PUMP UP	
MORNING MEDITATION	**READ 10 - 15 MIN**

AFFIRMATIONS
1
2
3

TOP THREE		

SCHEDULE			CALLS TO MAKE
			EMAILS TO WRITE
			NOTES

Seller Profile

CLIENT 1 - MR / MRS	
ADDRESS	**PHONE #**
	EMAIL

CLIENT 2 - MR / MRS	
ADDRESS	**PHONE #**
	EMAIL

LISTING DETAILS

LISTING APPOINTMENT	☐	☐	☐

SUGGESTED LISTING PRICE RANGE

BEDROOMS	**BATHS**	**SQUARE FOOTAGE**

DETAILS

MORTGAGE BALANCE	**INTEREST RATE**
LIENS	**HOA FEES**

TITLE COMPANY

NAME

COMPANY

PHONE	**FAX**	**EMAIL**

COOPERATING AGENT

NAME

COMPANY

PHONE	**FAX**	**EMAIL**

NOTES

Prospecting Contacts

NAME			PHONE NUMBER #
BUYER	SELLER	OTHER	PHONE NUMBER #
ADDRESS			APPOINTMENT INFO
			FOLLOW UP
NOTES			

NAME			PHONE NUMBER #
BUYER	SELLER	OTHER	PHONE NUMBER #
			APPOINTMENT INFO
			FOLLOW UP
NOTES			

NAME			PHONE NUMBER #
BUYER	SELLER	OTHER	PHONE NUMBER #
			APPOINTMENT INFO
			FOLLOW UP
NOTES			

NAME			PHONE NUMBER #
BUYER	SELLER	OTHER	PHONE NUMBER #
			APPOINTMENT INFO
			FOLLOW UP
NOTES			

Vision Board

"Vision without a task is only a dream. A task without a vision is but drudgery. But vision with a task is a dream fulfilled."– Anonymous

Prospecting Worksheet

DATE

START TIME   END TIME

CALL TRACKING

| X | CONTACT MADE | 0 | PROSPECT FOLLOW UP | ✓ | APPT. SCHEDULED |

☐ ☐ ☐ ☐ ☐ ☐ ☐ ☐ ☐ ☐ ☐ ☐ ☐ ☐ ☐ ☐

☐ ☐ ☐ ☐ ☐ ☐ ☐ ☐ ☐ ☐ ☐ ☐ ☐ ☐ ☐ ☐

☐ ☐ ☐ ☐ ☐ ☐ ☐ ☐ ☐ ☐ ☐ ☐ ☐ ☐ ☐ ☐

☐ ☐ ☐ ☐ ☐ ☐ ☐ ☐ ☐ ☐ ☐ ☐ ☐ ☐ ☐ ☐

CONTACTS

NAME	PHONE NUMBER #
BUYER SELLER OTHER	PHONE NUMBER #
ADDRESS	APPOINTMENT INFO
	FOLLOW UP
NOTES	

NAME	PHONE NUMBER #
BUYER SELLER OTHER	PHONE NUMBER #
	APPOINTMENT INFO
	FOLLOW UP
NOTES	

NAME	PHONE NUMBER #
BUYER SELLER OTHER	PHONE NUMBER #
	APPOINTMENT INFO
	FOLLOW UP
NOTES	

Goal Planning 2019

"No matter how many goals you have achieved, you must set your sights on a higher one" Jessica Savitchs

GOAL:

WHY IT'S MEANINGFUL:

HOW:

MONTHLY STEPS:

- ○
- ○
- ○
- ○
- ○
- ○

- ○
- ○
- ○
- ○
- ○
- ○

DAILY STEPS:

_____

_____

_____

_____

Goal Planning 2019

"Success is steady progress toward one's personal goals." - Jim Rohn

	NUMBER OF CLOSINGS	AVG COMMISSION PER CLOSING
FIRST 6 MONTHS		
LAST 6 MONTHS		

PROSPECTING GOALS

MARKETING GOALS

NETWORKING GOALS

PROFESSIONAL DEVELOPMENT GOALS

MONTH OF: July 2019

Goal Planning 2019

MONTHLY GOALS:

_____
_____
_____
_____

1 2 3 4 5

WEEKLY GOALS:

_____
_____
_____
_____
_____
_____

WHAT WORKED THIS MONTH

_____
_____
_____
_____
_____
_____
_____
_____

WHAT HAS NOT WORKED THIS MONTH

_____
_____
_____
_____
_____
_____
_____
_____

Closings Tracker

NAME	ADDRESS	DATE	AMOUNT

Buyer Profile

CLIENT 1 - MR / MRS		
ADDRESS	PHONE #	
	EMAIL	

CLIENT 2 - MR / MRS		
ADDRESS	PHONE #	
	EMAIL	

DETAILS		
PRICE RANGE	BEDROOMS	BATHS
AREAS		
MUST HAVES		
PREAPPROVED? YES	NO AMOUNT	
HOW THEY HEARD ABOUT ME		
CONTACT DATE	FOLLOW UP DATE	
CONTACT DATE	FOLLOW UP DATE	

LENDER CONTACT		
NAME		
COMPANY		
PHONE	FAX	EMAIL

TITLE COMPANY		
NAME		
COMPANY		
PHONE	FAX	EMAIL

COOPERATING AGENT		
NAME		
COMPANY		
PHONE	FAX	EMAIL

Backward Goal Setting

Work backwards from your ultimate goal and figure out what you need to get you there.

GOAL FOR SOMEDAY:
What's your ulitmate goal?

FIVE - YEAR GOAL:
based on your goal above, what can you do in the next five years to get you closer to your goal?

ONE - YEAR GOAL:
based on your goal above, what can you do in the next year to get you closer to your goal?

MONTHLY GOAL:
based on your goal above, what can you do in the next month to get you closer to your goal?

WEEKLY GOAL:
based on your goal above, what can you do in the next week to get you closer to your goal?

DAILY GOAL:
based on your goal above, what can you do today to get you closer to your goal?

GOAL FOR RIGHT NOW:
based on your goal above, what can you do right now?

DELISHA BOYD LLC

Event Sign In Sheet

NAME: _____

EMAIL: _____

PHONE: _____

ARE YOU PRE-QUALIFIED?
YES   NO
ARE YOU WORKING WITH AN AGENT?
YES   NO

NAME: _____

EMAIL: _____

PHONE: _____

ARE YOU PRE-QUALIFIED?
YES   NO
ARE YOU WORKING WITH AN AGENT?
YES   NO

NAME: _____

EMAIL: _____

PHONE: _____

ARE YOU PRE-QUALIFIED?
YES   NO
ARE YOU WORKING WITH AN AGENT?
YES   NO

NAME: _____

EMAIL: _____

PHONE: _____

ARE YOU PRE-QUALIFIED?
YES   NO
ARE YOU WORKING WITH AN AGENT?
YES   NO

NAME: _____

EMAIL: _____

PHONE: _____

ARE YOU PRE-QUALIFIED?
YES   NO
ARE YOU WORKING WITH AN AGENT?
YES   NO

NAME: _____

EMAIL: _____

PHONE: _____

ARE YOU PRE-QUALIFIED?
YES   NO
ARE YOU WORKING WITH AN AGENT?
YES   NO

NAME: _____

EMAIL: _____

PHONE: _____

ARE YOU PRE-QUALIFIED?
YES   NO
ARE YOU WORKING WITH AN AGENT?
YES   NO

Daily Ritual

DATE

MORNING PUMP UP	
MORNING MEDITATION	READ 10 - 15 MIN

AFFIRMATIONS

1	
2	
3	

TOP THREE

SCHEDULE			CALLS TO MAKE
			EMAILS TO WRITE
			NOTES

Seller Profile

CLIENT 1 - MR / MRS	
ADDRESS	**PHONE #**
	EMAIL
CLIENT 2 - MR / MRS	
ADDRESS	**PHONE #**
	EMAIL

LISTING DETAILS		
LISTING APPOINTMENT ☐	☐	☐
SUGGESTED LISTING PRICE RANGE		
BEDROOMS	**BATHS**	**SQUARE FOOTAGE**
DETAILS		
MORTGAGE BALANCE		**INTEREST RATE**
LIENS		**HOA FEES**

TITLE COMPANY		
NAME		
COMPANY		
PHONE	**FAX**	**EMAIL**

COOPERATING AGENT		
NAME		
COMPANY		
PHONE	**FAX**	**EMAIL**

NOTES

Prospecting Contacts

NAME	PHONE NUMBER #
BUYER SELLER OTHER	PHONE NUMBER #
ADDRESS	APPOINTMENT INFO
	FOLLOW UP
NOTES	

NAME	PHONE NUMBER #
BUYER SELLER OTHER	PHONE NUMBER #
	APPOINTMENT INFO
	FOLLOW UP
NOTES	

NAME	PHONE NUMBER #
BUYER SELLER OTHER	PHONE NUMBER #
	APPOINTMENT INFO
	FOLLOW UP
NOTES	

NAME	PHONE NUMBER #
BUYER SELLER OTHER	PHONE NUMBER #
	APPOINTMENT INFO
	FOLLOW UP
NOTES	

Vision Board

"The future belongs to those who see possibilities before they become obvious."
– John Scully

Prospecting Worksheet

CALL TRACKING		
X CONTACT MADE	**O** PROSPECT FOLLOW UP	**✓** APPT. SCHEDULED

☐ ☐ ☐ ☐ ☐ ☐ ☐ ☐ ☐ ☐ ☐ ☐ ☐ ☐ ☐ ☐ ☐ ☐

☐ ☐ ☐ ☐ ☐ ☐ ☐ ☐ ☐ ☐ ☐ ☐ ☐ ☐ ☐ ☐ ☐ ☐

☐ ☐ ☐ ☐ ☐ ☐ ☐ ☐ ☐ ☐ ☐ ☐ ☐ ☐ ☐ ☐ ☐ ☐

☐ ☐ ☐ ☐ ☐ ☐ ☐ ☐ ☐ ☐ ☐ ☐ ☐ ☐ ☐ ☐ ☐ ☐

CONTACTS

NAME			PHONE NUMBER #
BUYER	SELLER	OTHER	PHONE NUMBER #
ADDRESS			APPOINTMENT INFO
			FOLLOW UP
NOTES			

NAME			PHONE NUMBER #
BUYER	SELLER	OTHER	PHONE NUMBER #
			APPOINTMENT INFO
			FOLLOW UP
NOTES			

NAME			PHONE NUMBER #
BUYER	SELLER	OTHER	PHONE NUMBER #
			APPOINTMENT INFO
			FOLLOW UP
NOTES			

Goal Planning 2019

"Success is the progressive realization of predetermined, worthwhile, personal goals."
Paul J Meyer

GOAL:

WHY IT'S MEANINGFUL:

HOW:

MONTHLY STEPS:

- ○
- ○
- ○
- ○
- ○
- ○

- ○
- ○
- ○
- ○
- ○
- ○

DAILY STEPS:

_____
_____
_____
_____

_____
_____
_____
_____

Goal Planning 2019

"If you are not making the progress that you would like to make and are capable of making, it is simply because your goals are not clearly defined" - Paul Meyer

	NUMBER OF CLOSINGS	AVG COMMISSION PER CLOSING
FIRST 6 MONTHS		
LAST 6 MONTHS		

PROSPECTING GOALS

MARKETING GOALS

NETWORKING GOALS

PROFESSIONAL DEVELOPMENT GOALS

MONTH OF: August 2019

Goal Planning 2019

MONTHLY GOALS:

_____

_____

_____

_____

1   2   3   4   5

WEEKLY GOALS:

_____

_____

_____

_____

_____

_____

WHAT WORKED THIS MONTH

_____

_____

_____

_____

_____

_____

_____

_____

_____

_____

WHAT HAS NOT WORKED THIS MONTH

_____

_____

_____

_____

_____

_____

_____

_____

_____

_____

Closings Tracker

NAME	ADDRESS	DATE	AMOUNT

Buyer Profile

CLIENT 1 - MR / MRS	
ADDRESS	**PHONE #**
	EMAIL
CLIENT 2 - MR / MRS	
ADDRESS	**PHONE #**
	EMAIL

DETAILS

PRICE RANGE	**BEDROOMS**	**BATHS**
AREAS		
MUST HAVES		
PREAPPROVED? YES	NO **AMOUNT**	
HOW THEY HEARD ABOUT ME		
CONTACT DATE	**FOLLOW UP DATE**	
CONTACT DATE	**FOLLOW UP DATE**	

LENDER CONTACT

NAME		
COMPANY		
PHONE	**FAX**	**EMAIL**

TITLE COMPANY

NAME		
COMPANY		
PHONE	**FAX**	**EMAIL**

COOPERATING AGENT

NAME		
COMPANY		
PHONE	**FAX**	**EMAIL**

Backward Goal Setting

Work backwards from your ultimate goal and figure out what you need to get you there.

GOAL FOR SOMEDAY:
What's your ulitmate goal?

FIVE - YEAR GOAL:
based on your goal above, what can you do in the next five years to get you closer to your goal?

ONE - YEAR GOAL:
based on your goal above, what can you do in the next year to get you closer to your goal?

MONTHLY GOAL:
based on your goal above, what can you do in the next month to get you closer to your goal?

WEEKLY GOAL:
based on your goal above, what can you do in the next week to get you closer to your goal?

DAILY GOAL:
based on your goal above, what can you do today to get you closer to your goal?

GOAL FOR RIGHT NOW:
based on your goal above, what can you do right now?

Event Sign In Sheet

NAME: _____

EMAIL: _____

PHONE: _____

ARE YOU PRE-QUALIFIED?
    ☐ YES   ☐ NO
ARE YOU WORKING WITH AN AGENT?
    ☐ YES   ☐ NO

NAME: _____

EMAIL: _____

PHONE: _____

ARE YOU PRE-QUALIFIED?
    ☐ YES   ☐ NO
ARE YOU WORKING WITH AN AGENT?
    ☐ YES   ☐ NO

NAME: _____

EMAIL: _____

PHONE: _____

ARE YOU PRE-QUALIFIED?
    ☐ YES   ☐ NO
ARE YOU WORKING WITH AN AGENT?
    ☐ YES   ☐ NO

NAME: _____

EMAIL: _____

PHONE: _____

ARE YOU PRE-QUALIFIED?
    ☐ YES   ☐ NO
ARE YOU WORKING WITH AN AGENT?
    ☐ YES   ☐ NO

NAME: _____

EMAIL: _____

PHONE: _____

ARE YOU PRE-QUALIFIED?
    ☐ YES   ☐ NO
ARE YOU WORKING WITH AN AGENT?
    ☐ YES   ☐ NO

NAME: _____

EMAIL: _____

PHONE: _____

ARE YOU PRE-QUALIFIED?
    ☐ YES   ☐ NO
ARE YOU WORKING WITH AN AGENT?
    ☐ YES   ☐ NO

NAME: _____

EMAIL: _____

PHONE: _____

ARE YOU PRE-QUALIFIED?
    ☐ YES   ☐ NO
ARE YOU WORKING WITH AN AGENT?
    ☐ YES   ☐ NO

Daily Ritual

DATE

MORNING PUMP UP	
MORNING MEDITATION	READ 10 - 15 MIN

AFFIRMATIONS
1
2
3

TOP THREE		

SCHEDULE			CALLS TO MAKE
			EMAILS TO WRITE
			NOTES

Seller Profile

CLIENT 1 - MR / MRS	
ADDRESS	**PHONE #**
	EMAIL
CLIENT 2 - MR / MRS	
ADDRESS	**PHONE #**
	EMAIL

LISTING DETAILS		
LISTING APPOINTMENT ☐	☐	☐
SUGGESTED LISTING PRICE RANGE		
BEDROOMS	**BATHS**	**SQUARE FOOTAGE**
DETAILS		
MORTGAGE BALANCE		**INTEREST RATE**
LIENS		**HOA FEES**

TITLE COMPANY		
NAME		
COMPANY		
PHONE	**FAX**	**EMAIL**

COOPERATING AGENT		
NAME		
COMPANY		
PHONE	**FAX**	**EMAIL**

NOTES

Prospecting Contacts

NAME	PHONE NUMBER #
BUYER SELLER OTHER	PHONE NUMBER #
ADDRESS	APPOINTMENT INFO
	FOLLOW UP
NOTES	

NAME	PHONE NUMBER #
BUYER SELLER OTHER	PHONE NUMBER #
	APPOINTMENT INFO
	FOLLOW UP
NOTES	

NAME	PHONE NUMBER #
BUYER SELLER OTHER	PHONE NUMBER #
	APPOINTMENT INFO
	FOLLOW UP
NOTES	

NAME	PHONE NUMBER #
BUYER SELLER OTHER	PHONE NUMBER #
	APPOINTMENT INFO
	FOLLOW UP
NOTES	

Vision Board

"A vision is not just a picture of what could be; it is an appeal to our better selves, a call to become something more." – Rosabeth Moss Kanter

Prospecting Worksheet

CALL TRACKING

X CONTACT MADE	0 PROSPECT FOLLOW UP	✓ APPT. SCHEDULED

CONTACTS

NAME	PHONE NUMBER #
BUYER SELLER OTHER	PHONE NUMBER #
ADDRESS	APPOINTMENT INFO
	FOLLOW UP
NOTES	

NAME	PHONE NUMBER #
BUYER SELLER OTHER	PHONE NUMBER #
	APPOINTMENT INFO
	FOLLOW UP
NOTES	

NAME	PHONE NUMBER #
BUYER SELLER OTHER	PHONE NUMBER #
	APPOINTMENT INFO
	FOLLOW UP
NOTES	

Goal Planning 2019

"Goals give us purpose, which, in turn, motivates us to make ourselves the best version in all aspects of your life." Hannah Bronfman

GOAL:

WHY IT'S MEANINGFUL:

HOW:

MONTHLY STEPS:

○
○

○
○

○
○

○
○

○
○

○
○

DAILY STEPS:

_____   _____

_____   _____

_____   _____

_____   _____

Goal Planning 2019

"If you want to accomplish the goals of your life, you have to begin with the spirit."
Oprah Winfrey

	NUMBER OF CLOSINGS	AVG COMMISSION PER CLOSING
FIRST 6 MONTHS		
LAST 6 MONTHS		

PROSPECTING GOALS

MARKETING GOALS

NETWORKING GOALS

PROFESSIONAL DEVELOPMENT GOALS

Goal Planning 2019

MONTHLY GOALS:

_____
_____
_____
_____

1 2 3 4 5

WEEKLY GOALS:

_____
_____
_____
_____
_____
_____
_____

WHAT WORKED THIS MONTH

_____
_____
_____
_____
_____
_____
_____
_____
_____
_____

WHAT HAS NOT WORKED THIS MONTH

_____
_____
_____
_____
_____
_____
_____
_____
_____
_____

Closings Tracker

NAME	ADDRESS	DATE	AMOUNT

Buyer Profile

CLIENT 1 - MR / MRS	
ADDRESS	PHONE #
	EMAIL

CLIENT 2 - MR / MRS	
ADDRESS	PHONE #
	EMAIL

DETAILS

PRICE RANGE	BEDROOMS	BATHS
AREAS		
MUST HAVES		
PREAPPROVED? YES NO AMOUNT		
HOW THEY HEARD ABOUT ME		
CONTACT DATE	FOLLOW UP DATE	
CONTACT DATE	FOLLOW UP DATE	

LENDER CONTACT

NAME		
COMPANY		
PHONE	FAX	EMAIL

TITLE COMPANY

NAME		
COMPANY		
PHONE	FAX	EMAIL

COOPERATING AGENT

NAME		
COMPANY		
PHONE	FAX	EMAIL

Backward Goal Setting

Work backwards from your ultimate goal and figure out what you need to get you there.

GOAL FOR SOMEDAY:
What's your ulitmate goal?

FIVE - YEAR GOAL:
based on your goal above, what can you do in the next five years to get you closer to your goal?

ONE - YEAR GOAL:
based on your goal above, what can you do in the next year to get you closer to your goal?

MONTHLY GOAL:
based on your goal above, what can you do in the next month to get you closer to your goal?

WEEKLY GOAL:
based on your goal above, what can you do in the next week to get you closer to your goal?

DAILY GOAL:
based on your goal above, what can you do today to get you closer to your goal?

GOAL FOR RIGHT NOW:
based on your goal above, what can you do right now?

DELISHA BOYD LLC

Event Sign In Sheet

NAME: _____

EMAIL: _____

PHONE: _____

ARE YOU PRE-QUALIFIED?
☐ YES   ☐ NO
ARE YOU WORKING WITH AN AGENT?
☐ YES   ☐ NO

NAME: _____

EMAIL: _____

PHONE: _____

ARE YOU PRE-QUALIFIED?
☐ YES   ☐ NO
ARE YOU WORKING WITH AN AGENT?
☐ YES   ☐ NO

NAME: _____

EMAIL: _____

PHONE: _____

ARE YOU PRE-QUALIFIED?
☐ YES   ☐ NO
ARE YOU WORKING WITH AN AGENT?
☐ YES   ☐ NO

NAME: _____

EMAIL: _____

PHONE: _____

ARE YOU PRE-QUALIFIED?
☐ YES   ☐ NO
ARE YOU WORKING WITH AN AGENT?
☐ YES   ☐ NO

NAME: _____

EMAIL: _____

PHONE: _____

ARE YOU PRE-QUALIFIED?
☐ YES   ☐ NO
ARE YOU WORKING WITH AN AGENT?
☐ YES   ☐ NO

NAME: _____

EMAIL: _____

PHONE: _____

ARE YOU PRE-QUALIFIED?
☐ YES   ☐ NO
ARE YOU WORKING WITH AN AGENT?
☐ YES   ☐ NO

NAME: _____

EMAIL: _____

PHONE: _____

ARE YOU PRE-QUALIFIED?
☐ YES   ☐ NO
ARE YOU WORKING WITH AN AGENT?
☐ YES   ☐ NO

Daily Ritual

DATE

MORNING PUMP UP	
MORNING MEDITATION	**READ 10 - 15 MIN**

AFFIRMATIONS	
1	
2	
3	

TOP THREE		

SCHEDULE			CALLS TO MAKE
			EMAILS TO WRITE
			NOTES

Seller Profile

CLIENT 1 - MR / MRS	
ADDRESS	**PHONE #**
	EMAIL
CLIENT 2 - MR / MRS	
ADDRESS	**PHONE #**
	EMAIL

LISTING DETAILS		
LISTING APPOINTMENT ☐	☐	☐
SUGGESTED LISTING PRICE RANGE		
BEDROOMS	**BATHS**	**SQUARE FOOTAGE**
DETAILS		
MORTGAGE BALANCE		**INTEREST RATE**
LIENS		**HOA FEES**

TITLE COMPANY		
NAME		
COMPANY		
PHONE	**FAX**	**EMAIL**

COOPERATING AGENT		
NAME		
COMPANY		
PHONE	**FAX**	**EMAIL**

NOTES

Prospecting Contacts

NAME			PHONE NUMBER #
BUYER	SELLER	OTHER	PHONE NUMBER #
ADDRESS			APPOINTMENT INFO
			FOLLOW UP
NOTES			

NAME			PHONE NUMBER #
BUYER	SELLER	OTHER	PHONE NUMBER #
			APPOINTMENT INFO
			FOLLOW UP
NOTES			

NAME			PHONE NUMBER #
BUYER	SELLER	OTHER	PHONE NUMBER #
			APPOINTMENT INFO
			FOLLOW UP
NOTES			

NAME			PHONE NUMBER #
BUYER	SELLER	OTHER	PHONE NUMBER #
			APPOINTMENT INFO
			FOLLOW UP
NOTES			

Vision Board

"Leadership is the capacity to translate vision into reality." – Warren Bennis

"Leadership is the capacity to translate vision into reality." – Warren Bennis

Prospecting Worksheet

DATE

START TIME   **END TIME**

CALL TRACKING

X	CONTACT MADE	O	PROSPECT FOLLOW UP	✓	APPT. SCHEDULED

CONTACTS

NAME	PHONE NUMBER #
BUYER SELLER OTHER	PHONE NUMBER #
ADDRESS	APPOINTMENT INFO
	FOLLOW UP
NOTES	

NAME	PHONE NUMBER #
BUYER SELLER OTHER	PHONE NUMBER #
	APPOINTMENT INFO
	FOLLOW UP
NOTES	

NAME	PHONE NUMBER #
BUYER SELLER OTHER	PHONE NUMBER #
	APPOINTMENT INFO
	FOLLOW UP
NOTES	

Goal Planning 2019

"Goals allow you to control the direction of change in your favor." - Brian Tracy

GOAL:

WHY IT'S MEANINGFUL:

HOW:

MONTHLY STEPS:

- ○
- ○
- ○
- ○
- ○
- ○

- ○
- ○
- ○
- ○
- ○
- ○

DAILY STEPS:

_____   _____

_____   _____

_____   _____

_____   _____

Goal Planning 2019

"There's nothing wrong with being driven. And there's nothing wrong with putting yourself first to reach your goals." Shonda Rhimes

	NUMBER OF CLOSINGS	AVG COMMISSION PER CLOSING
FIRST 6 MONTHS		
LAST 6 MONTHS		

PROSPECTING GOALS

MARKETING GOALS

NETWORKING GOALS

PROFESSIONAL DEVELOPMENT GOALS

MONTH OF: October 2019

Goal Planning 2019

MONTHLY GOALS:

_____
_____
_____
_____

1   2   3   4   5

WEEKLY GOALS:

_____
_____
_____
_____
_____
_____

WHAT WORKED THIS MONTH

_____
_____
_____
_____
_____
_____
_____
_____
_____

WHAT HAS NOT WORKED THIS MONTH

_____
_____
_____
_____
_____
_____
_____
_____
_____

Closings Tracker

NAME	ADDRESS	DATE	AMOUNT

Buyer Profile

CLIENT 1 - MR / MRS	
ADDRESS	PHONE #
	EMAIL

CLIENT 2 - MR / MRS	
ADDRESS	PHONE #
	EMAIL

DETAILS

PRICE RANGE	BEDROOMS	BATHS
AREAS		
MUST HAVES		
PREAPPROVED? YES NO AMOUNT		
HOW THEY HEARD ABOUT ME		
CONTACT DATE	FOLLOW UP DATE	
CONTACT DATE	FOLLOW UP DATE	

LENDER CONTACT

NAME		
COMPANY		
PHONE	FAX	EMAIL

TITLE COMPANY

NAME		
COMPANY		
PHONE	FAX	EMAIL

COOPERATING AGENT

NAME		
COMPANY		
PHONE	FAX	EMAIL

Backward Goal Setting

Work backwards from your ultimate goal and figure out what you need to get you there.

GOAL FOR SOMEDAY:
What's your ulitmate goal?

FIVE - YEAR GOAL:
based on your goal above, what can you do in the next five years to get you closer to your goal?

ONE - YEAR GOAL:
based on your goal above, what can you do in the next year to get you closer to your goal?

MONTHLY GOAL:
based on your goal above, what can you do in the next month to get you closer to your goal?

WEEKLY GOAL:
based on your goal above, what can you do in the next week to get you closer to your goal?

DAILY GOAL:
based on your goal above, what can you do today to get you closer to your goal?

GOAL FOR RIGHT NOW:
based on your goal above, what can you do right now?

Event Sign In Sheet

NAME: _____

EMAIL: _____

PHONE: _____

ARE YOU PRE-QUALIFIED?
YES   NO
ARE YOU WORKING WITH AN AGENT?
YES   NO

NAME: _____

EMAIL: _____

PHONE: _____

ARE YOU PRE--QUALIFIED?
YES   NO
ARE YOU WORKING WITH AN AGENT?
YES   NO

NAME: _____

EMAIL: _____

PHONE: _____

ARE YOU PRE-QUALIFIED?
YES   NO
ARE YOU WORKING WITH AN AGENT?
YES   NO

NAME: _____

EMAIL: _____

PHONE: _____

ARE YOU PRE-QUALIFIED?
YES   NO
ARE YOU WORKING WITH AN AGENT?
YES   NO

NAME: _____

EMAIL: _____

PHONE: _____

ARE YOU PRE-QUALIFIED?
YES   NO
ARE YOU WORKING WITH AN AGENT?
YES   NO

NAME: _____

EMAIL: _____

PHONE: _____

ARE YOU PRE-QUALIFIED?
YES   NO
ARE YOU WORKING WITH AN AGENT?
YES   NO

NAME: _____

EMAIL: _____

PHONE: _____

ARE YOU PRE-QUALIFIED?
YES   NO
ARE YOU WORKING WITH AN AGENT?
YES   NO

Daily Ritual

DATE

MORNING PUMP UP	
MORNING MEDITATION	**READ 10 - 15 MIN**

AFFIRMATIONS	
1	
2	
3	

TOP THREE		

SCHEDULE			CALLS TO MAKE
			EMAILS TO WRITE
			NOTES

Seller Profile

CLIENT 1 - MR / MRS	
ADDRESS	PHONE #
	EMAIL

CLIENT 2 - MR / MRS	
ADDRESS	PHONE #
	EMAIL

LISTING DETAILS

LISTING APPOINTMENT	☐	☐	☐

SUGGESTED LISTING PRICE RANGE		
BEDROOMS	BATHS	SQUARE FOOTAGE
DETAILS		
MORTGAGE BALANCE		INTEREST RATE
LIENS		HOA FEES

TITLE COMPANY

NAME		
COMPANY		
PHONE	FAX	EMAIL

COOPERATING AGENT

NAME		
COMPANY		
PHONE	FAX	EMAIL

NOTES

Prospecting Contacts

NAME			PHONE NUMBER #
BUYER	SELLER	OTHER	PHONE NUMBER #
ADDRESS			APPOINTMENT INFO
			FOLLOW UP
NOTES			

NAME			PHONE NUMBER #
BUYER	SELLER	OTHER	PHONE NUMBER #
			APPOINTMENT INFO
			FOLLOW UP
NOTES			

NAME			PHONE NUMBER #
BUYER	SELLER	OTHER	PHONE NUMBER #
			APPOINTMENT INFO
			FOLLOW UP
NOTES			

NAME			PHONE NUMBER #
BUYER	SELLER	OTHER	PHONE NUMBER #
			APPOINTMENT INFO
			FOLLOW UP
NOTES			

Vision Board

"If you create the vision for your life, DOORS WILL OPEN" - Anonymous

Prospecting Worksheet

DATE

START TIME   END TIME

CALL TRACKING		
✗ CONTACT MADE	𝘖 PROSPECT FOLLOW UP	✓ APPT. SCHEDULED

☐ ☐ ☐ ☐ ☐ ☐ ☐ ☐ ☐ ☐ ☐ ☐ ☐ ☐ ☐ ☐

☐ ☐ ☐ ☐ ☐ ☐ ☐ ☐ ☐ ☐ ☐ ☐ ☐ ☐ ☐ ☐

☐ ☐ ☐ ☐ ☐ ☐ ☐ ☐ ☐ ☐ ☐ ☐ ☐ ☐ ☐ ☐

☐ ☐ ☐ ☐ ☐ ☐ ☐ ☐ ☐ ☐ ☐ ☐ ☐ ☐ ☐ ☐

CONTACTS

NAME			PHONE NUMBER #
BUYER	SELLER	OTHER	PHONE NUMBER #
ADDRESS			APPOINTMENT INFO
			FOLLOW UP
NOTES			

NAME			PHONE NUMBER #
BUYER	SELLER	OTHER	PHONE NUMBER #
			APPOINTMENT INFO
			FOLLOW UP
NOTES			

NAME			PHONE NUMBER #
BUYER	SELLER	OTHER	PHONE NUMBER #
			APPOINTMENT INFO
			FOLLOW UP
NOTES			

Goal Planning 2019

"Decide who you are and what your goals entail - then go for the roses. Life has little regard for those who waste time." Jon Huntsman Sr

GOAL:

WHY IT'S MEANINGFUL:

HOW:

MONTHLY STEPS:

- ○
- ○
- ○
- ○
- ○
- ○

- ○
- ○
- ○
- ○
- ○
- ○

DAILY STEPS:

_____   _____

_____   _____

_____   _____

_____   _____

Goal Planning 2019

"Goals give you a mark to shoot for and keep you motivated when you face adversity"
Benjamin Watson

	NUMBER OF CLOSINGS	AVG COMMISSION PER CLOSING
FIRST 6 MONTHS		
LAST 6 MONTHS		

PROSPECTING GOALS

MARKETING GOALS

NETWORKING GOALS

PROFESSIONAL DEVELOPMENT GOALS

Goal Planning 2019

MONTHLY GOALS:

_____

_____

_____

_____

1 2 3 4 5

WEEKLY GOALS:

_____

_____

_____

_____

_____

_____

WHAT WORKED THIS MONTH

_____

_____

_____

_____

_____

_____

_____

_____

WHAT HAS NOT WORKED THIS MONTH

_____

_____

_____

_____

_____

_____

_____

_____

Closings Tracker

NAME	ADDRESS	DATE	AMOUNT

Buyer Profile

CLIENT 1 - MR / MRS		
ADDRESS	PHONE #	
	EMAIL	

CLIENT 2 - MR / MRS		
ADDRESS	PHONE #	
	EMAIL	

DETAILS		
PRICE RANGE	BEDROOMS	BATHS
AREAS		
MUST HAVES		
PREAPPROVED? YES	NO AMOUNT	
HOW THEY HEARD ABOUT ME		
CONTACT DATE	FOLLOW UP DATE	
CONTACT DATE	FOLLOW UP DATE	

LENDER CONTACT		
NAME		
COMPANY		
PHONE	FAX	EMAIL

TITLE COMPANY		
NAME		
COMPANY		
PHONE	FAX	EMAIL

COOPERATING AGENT		
NAME		
COMPANY		
PHONE	FAX	EMAIL

Backward Goal Setting

Work backwards from your ultimate goal and figure out what you need to get you there.

GOAL FOR SOMEDAY:
What's your ulitmate goal?

FIVE - YEAR GOAL:
based on your goal above, what can you do in the next five years to get you closer to your goal?

ONE - YEAR GOAL:
based on your goal above, what can you do in the next year to get you closer to your goal?

MONTHLY GOAL:
based on your goal above, what can you do in the next month to get you closer to your goal?

WEEKLY GOAL:
based on your goal above, what can you do in the next week to get you closer to your goal?

DAILY GOAL:
based on your goal above, what can you do today to get you closer to your goal?

GOAL FOR RIGHT NOW:
based on your goal above, what can you do right now?

DELISHA BOYD LLC

Event Sign In Sheet

NAME: _____

EMAIL: _____

PHONE: _____

ARE YOU PRE-QUALIFIED?

☐ YES   ☐ NO

ARE YOU WORKING WITH AN AGENT?

☐ YES   ☐ NO

NAME: _____

EMAIL: _____

PHONE: _____

ARE YOU PRE-QUALIFIED?

☐ YES   ☐ NO

ARE YOU WORKING WITH AN AGENT?

☐ YES   ☐ NO

NAME: _____

EMAIL: _____

PHONE: _____

ARE YOU PRE-QUALIFIED?

☐ YES   ☐ NO

ARE YOU WORKING WITH AN AGENT?

☐ YES   ☐ NO

NAME: _____

EMAIL: _____

PHONE: _____

ARE YOU PRE-QUALIFIED?

☐ YES   ☐ NO

ARE YOU WORKING WITH AN AGENT?

☐ YES   ☐ NO

NAME: _____

EMAIL: _____

PHONE: _____

ARE YOU PRE-QUALIFIED?

☐ YES   ☐ NO

ARE YOU WORKING WITH AN AGENT?

☐ YES   ☐ NO

NAME: _____

EMAIL: _____

PHONE: _____

ARE YOU PRE-QUALIFIED?

☐ YES   ☐ NO

ARE YOU WORKING WITH AN AGENT?

☐ YES   ☐ NO

NAME: _____

EMAIL: _____

PHONE: _____

ARE YOU PRE-QUALIFIED?

☐ YES   ☐ NO

ARE YOU WORKING WITH AN AGENT?

☐ YES   ☐ NO

Daily Ritual

DATE

MORNING PUMP UP	
MORNING MEDITATION	READ 10 - 15 MIN

AFFIRMATIONS	
1	
2	
3	

TOP THREE

SCHEDULE		CALLS TO MAKE
		EMAILS TO WRITE
		NOTES

Seller Profile

CLIENT 1 - MR / MRS	
ADDRESS	**PHONE #**
	EMAIL

CLIENT 2 - MR / MRS	
ADDRESS	**PHONE #**
	EMAIL

LISTING DETAILS

LISTING APPOINTMENT ☐	☐	☐
SUGGESTED LISTING PRICE RANGE		
BEDROOMS	**BATHS**	**SQUARE FOOTAGE**
DETAILS		
MORTGAGE BALANCE		**INTEREST RATE**
LIENS		**HOA FEES**

TITLE COMPANY

NAME		
COMPANY		
PHONE	**FAX**	**EMAIL**

COOPERATING AGENT

NAME		
COMPANY		
PHONE	**FAX**	**EMAIL**

NOTES

Prospecting Contacts

NAME	PHONE NUMBER #
BUYER SELLER OTHER	PHONE NUMBER #
ADDRESS	APPOINTMENT INFO
	FOLLOW UP
NOTES	

NAME	PHONE NUMBER #
BUYER SELLER OTHER	PHONE NUMBER #
	APPOINTMENT INFO
	FOLLOW UP
NOTES	

NAME	PHONE NUMBER #
BUYER SELLER OTHER	PHONE NUMBER #
	APPOINTMENT INFO
	FOLLOW UP
NOTES	

NAME	PHONE NUMBER #
BUYER SELLER OTHER	PHONE NUMBER #
	APPOINTMENT INFO
	FOLLOW UP
NOTES	

Vision Board

"Vision without action is merely a dream." - Joel Barker

Prospecting Worksheet

DATE

START TIME   END TIME

CALL TRACKING

X CONTACT MADE	O PROSPECT FOLLOW UP	✓ APPT. SCHEDULED

CONTACTS

NAME			PHONE NUMBER #
BUYER	SELLER	OTHER	PHONE NUMBER #
ADDRESS			APPOINTMENT INFO
			FOLLOW UP
NOTES			

NAME			PHONE NUMBER #
BUYER	SELLER	OTHER	PHONE NUMBER #
			APPOINTMENT INFO
			FOLLOW UP
NOTES			

NAME			PHONE NUMBER #
BUYER	SELLER	OTHER	PHONE NUMBER #
			APPOINTMENT INFO
			FOLLOW UP
NOTES			

Goal Planning 2019

"Goals give us purpose, which, in turn, motivates us to make ourselves the best version in all aspects of your life." Hannah Bronfman

GOAL:

WHY IT'S MEANINGFUL:

HOW:

MONTHLY STEPS:

- ○
- ○
- ○
- ○
- ○
- ○

- ○
- ○
- ○
- ○
- ○
- ○

DAILY STEPS:

_____   _____

_____   _____

_____   _____

_____   _____

Goal Planning 2019

"Learn from the past, set vivid, detailed goals for the future, and live in the only moment of time over which you have any control: NOW" - Denis Waitley

	NUMBER OF CLOSINGS	AVG COMMISSION PER CLOSING
FIRST 6 MONTHS		
LAST 6 MONTHS		

PROSPECTING GOALS

MARKETING GOALS

NETWORKING GOALS

PROFESSIONAL DEVELOPMENT GOALS

Goal Planning 2019

MONTHLY GOALS:

_____

_____

_____

_____

1 2 3 4 5

WEEKLY GOALS:

_____

_____

_____

_____

_____

_____

WHAT WORKED THIS MONTH

_____

_____

_____

_____

_____

_____

_____

_____

WHAT HAS NOT WORKED THIS MONTH

_____

_____

_____

_____

_____

_____

_____

_____

Closings Tracker

NAME	ADDRESS	DATE	AMOUNT

Buyer Profile

CLIENT 1 - MR / MRS	
ADDRESS	**PHONE #**
	EMAIL

CLIENT 2 - MR / MRS	
ADDRESS	**PHONE #**
	EMAIL

DETAILS

PRICE RANGE	**BEDROOMS**	**BATHS**
AREAS		
MUST HAVES		
PREAPPROVED? YES	NO **AMOUNT**	
HOW THEY HEARD ABOUT ME		
CONTACT DATE	**FOLLOW UP DATE**	
CONTACT DATE	**FOLLOW UP DATE**	

LENDER CONTACT

NAME		
COMPANY		
PHONE	**FAX**	**EMAIL**

TITLE COMPANY

NAME		
COMPANY		
PHONE	**FAX**	**EMAIL**

COOPERATING AGENT

NAME		
COMPANY		
PHONE	**FAX**	**EMAIL**

Backward Goal Setting

Work backwards from your ultimate goal and figure out what you need to get you there.

GOAL FOR SOMEDAY:
What's your ulitmate goal?

FIVE - YEAR GOAL:
based on your goal above, what can you do in the next five years to get you closer to your goal?

ONE - YEAR GOAL:
based on your goal above, what can you do in the next year to get you closer to your goal?

MONTHLY GOAL:
based on your goal above, what can you do in the next month to get you closer to your goal?

WEEKLY GOAL:
based on your goal above, what can you do in the next week to get you closer to your goal?

DAILY GOAL:
based on your goal above, what can you do today to get you closer to your goal?

GOAL FOR RIGHT NOW:
based on your goal above, what can you do right now?

www.ingramcontent.com/pod-product-compliance
Lightning Source LLC
Chambersburg PA
CBHW081149180526
45170CB00006B/1996